HOW TO WEAR GRUNGE
RUTH STACEY

KFS
PAMPHLETS

Newton-le-Willows

Published in the United Kingdom in 2018
by The Knives Forks And Spoons Press,
51 Pipit Avenue,
Newton-le-Willows,
Merseyside,
WA12 9RG.

ISBN 978-1-912211-30-2

Acknowledgements:

Thank you to all my friends. You got me home alive. Mia Zapata lives and always will if you listen to her music.

Drinking song reproduced with permission from Steve Moriarty. Quotes or allusions included from Kerouac, Rimbaud, Rossetti, Shakespeare. *It's when the punctuation goes, you know you're high* published 2017 in The Interpreter's House magazine. *The Worst Thing* included in the #MeToo anthology, from Fairacre Press, edited by Deborah Alma.

In Memoriam to .... [blank for you to fill in]

Contents

I tend to drink too much sometimes
I fall a little drunk on my face
I get up I brush up I head to the bar
For another round with all of my friends
Here's to 'em! To all of my friends

– The Gits: Drinking Song

'Affect a street-sleeper aesthetic as if you have no choice but to wear worn-out clothes! Even though you can afford classier clothes act indifferently, as if you reject the material world! Look miserable & wear dark eye shadow!'

– Fashion advice for people wanting to,
'Wear the grunge look.'

First Seen Following a Link Online

Glimpsed through photographs unearthed from
forgotten boxes or left between the pages of a book,
a novel half read & discarded *striking* beauty
is beauty even if the subject is long dead: here
she is staring out of the monitor.

Who was she?

Ruth Stacey

Chant & Be Happy!

It wasn't all bad   not like the adverts said,
& that was why we distrusted the just
say no
        hypocrites in their pubs
addicted in their own way

let's be honest: all our worst nights were
drunk, or watching others drunk-angry

        we were in the soft field, folded
in each other's arms   we got in free
the stones were around us & we had
spent all our money on drugs as soon
as we arrived

high on the floor   looking down the fields
realising we had no money left
but still feeling we had our priorities right

we found a path to the Hare Krishna tent
& found ourselves pulled into the gloom
the red & yellow & chanting —
there was room for us

each morning & evening they fed us
for free & we listened to their words
repeating, generously enveloping

it wasn't just the drugs that made us
all feel love   *suffer*   it was each other

Who Was She?

Like opening a letter but the page is blank. Like hearing a knock at the door but when you pull it open there is only the wind passing by & the sound of a sparrow. Like the smell of scent on the hurrying train that reminds you of 20 years ago. Like something gone too soon. Like inarticulate rage that makes you cough & pant for breath. Burnt-wood coloured hair thrashes in the breeze.

Continue to find out who she was?

Respect a dead person & don't pry?

Her Name

She left a quickly scrawled business card, listing her attributes:
bright, witty, sexy, tenacious, generous,
irresistible, reckless, wild, petite biche

Name: Carey Hunter

Age: 20

Address: Somewhere familiar, cold snap in the air, city buzzing,
guitar music playing, lyrics aim & circle: theme gloom/not gloom.

Voice: Growl, low, high, light, whispered, bellowed, impossible
to describe. Butterfly made of paper, caught in the draft.

Eyes: Fox coloured. I'm certain, fox-russet, copper.

Smell: You can't smell her through the internet. Come on.

Was any of that true? (Be cynical, doubt the stories).

Don't Pry

Look, mysteries always end up layering on top of each other,
like reams of paper. You think you have unearthed a truth,
a chronicle of the past, a statement … but memories are faulty,
right? You talk to someone & say: do you remember when
& they recall a completely different scenario. The emotion
of the event tinges it a different colour, which spreads like
drops of paint on blotting paper. That dark intense memory,
the fade to calmer emotions. At the time: jealousy. Now it's
nostalgia. I always liked her, they say. Forgetting how much
she annoyed them, how much she took. Forgetting the cruel
things they said.

But I can't look away.

I want to know something new, something fresh.

Be Cynical, Doubt the Stories

'I was friends with her at High School, she was always pushing to be centre of attention. So skinny, but she had this personality! You couldn't ignore her. And determined, my God, was she determined and stubborn. Wild too. Hair, curly, hanging right down her back like a cape. I was a good girl, I mean I drank a bit but she was keen to slip out of the back and smoke weed, take stuff. Like she was on a fun-fair ride and even though it was broken and swaying, she wouldn't get off but kept rising higher and higher, even as we called out, 'Carey, come back down.'

Fresh Meat

An anecdote that reinforces your perceived impression
of her that fits your model of her that aligns your already
written play. Something witty. Something feisty. Something
that shows she really did love him. That their love was tragic
romantic, lost.

Yet, you don't even know her, you never heard her laugh.
This is a death cult, macabre crush, being interested in a girl
who died a long time ago because she was his muse.
Because the wildness reminds you of yourself, but you
weren't as committed as her. A shadow of a shadow.

Just stop it. Even if his music was the soundtrack
of your old days.

Not that, not vague, a real quote, a real story.

 Yes, more like this, lecture me some more.

Lecture to Myself

she was a real woman who died, why are you
obsessed with her anyway?
pretty, pretty, pretty
stare all day at pretty things
girls called Helen Helena Hello Hello
dark haired & sultry
boys with sad eyes & poetic *underfed* bones
a thing of beauty is a joy ... etc.
Keats knew the power of an unrequited thing
& you could say this is second-hand electric love
yes, you fall in love with people   you crush
intensity of falling chest compressed beneath the weight
crushing the real her away dust in the air
truth   she reminds you/me of a period of time
hippy wall hangings & live bands
smokes, pills, music   when nothing/everything hurt
drinking morning red wine into limb-splayed openness
wanting to screw her, him, them, everyone
dressing her up   twisting her   cut-out
paper doll   compress me again

Not that, not Vague, a Real Quote, a Real Story

There was a night she was falling out of the club, in a pile of hippy skirts
& mirrored waistcoat; light glinting off the orange street lights.
She had a habit of flashing her small tits at anyone, to make them blush,
surprise them, hell, just to see the flash of surprise in their eyes. She never
wore a bra so the air was always close to her, the temptation to lift her hem
& bare herself. She didn't care about what they thought. Perhaps, you can
analyse this? One night someone said something, a bet, & she answered:

> *I'd walk through the city topless for forty, through*
> *all the drunk people, the on-coming cars.*
> *Pay me & I'll do it, she said, lifting her top.*

The night air was leering & no one seemed to notice her nakedness,
like she had vanished entirely & was only a suggestion of a person.
Later, she listened to a copied tape of *The Winding Sheet* by Mark
Lanegan: rewinding it & playing it again & again & again
waiting to come down

> *Did that really happen?*

This sounds like poetry – are you tricking me into reading poetry?

Define Poetry

Seriously, tell me what a poem is
then we can work out if this collection
of words & images
is entertaining fluff or more.
Define poetry.
Does it have to rhyme to be
or just place the words with gaps

that leave space to see

        & feel/think.

I don't know. I just love words
(& pretty things) Rub this out, I mean,
you can apply Tipp-Ex or cut the words out
that you don't like. The lines that are too cliché.

        that sink below the water.
Virginia, you filled your pockets with stones:
some days I pick them up & fill
the spaces in my life with granite
so if I step into the water
I won't rise but *burn burn burn*
like fabulous

This is poetry, for sure:

Royalty

One fine morning, in a land of very gentle people, a superb man and woman were shouting in the public square. "Friends, I want her to be queen!" "I want to be queen!" She laughed and trembled. He spoke to his friends of revelation, of ordeals terminated. They leaned on each other in ecstasy.

They were indeed sovereigns for a whole morning, while all the houses were adorned with crimson hangings, and for an entire afternoon, while they made their way toward the palm gardens.

–Arthur Rimbaud
Translated by Louise Varèse 1946

Is it? It's all rather teenage with Dali pinned to wall.

Rimbaud? Really? You'll say you love Jim Morrison next.

Did that Really Happen?

Yes. It happened in my life, to me.
Although I'm remembering
     through a fog.

I was actually wearing flared
jeans & battered Vans
that fit like slippers.

    So I can't trust anything you say?

But I Can't Look Away

She was so pretty.
She was so unique.
She wore clothes so well.
She was slender-limbed like a deer.
She had the greatest smile.
She was the *love my girl* of a talented man.
She hung around with rock stars.
She was the muse of the singer who calms me.
She was a groupie.
She loved drugs that made everything beautiful.
She made this list past tense.
She reminds me of my own reckless past.
~~She loved Jim Morrison.~~ Cut this line
She cleansed the doors of perception.
Did everything appear as it truly was?

Give me another list.

Describe a picture that no else has seen.

It's When the Punctuation Goes, You Know You're High

        sat in the cellar club toilet, red walls
graffiti on every surface
calm oasis in the madness/

bodies packed in skin ignites
        regular dealer holding court
bearded dandy   skinny & paranoid
insert any punctuation --- here ****

        em dash there eyes focused then blurred
what   % does   that   say?

& words/ words are my everything
& these can't be genuine:
who would write that?
just to melt my mind/*
(I like the names of punctuation:
parentheses, ellipses, hyphen &
the finest one is ampersand)

I drag someone in there & she can't see
it, but it is there, beneath the paint
scratched into the wood/ I adore
my owl named
Marvin/

        O true apothecary! Thy drugs are quick

How to Wear Grunge

with big inside pockets for wine
      bottles to drink on
      your come down
with layers to keep you warm
with borrowed nonchalance
with charity shop stalking
with delight at finding a hoodie
      at Bill O'Driscoll's bedsit
      then avoiding the girl
      who owned it
with slyness & light fingers
with sneak
with detachment
with the blur of smoke
with blim burns
with ripped flares
with friendship bands
with familiarity & comfort
      burying under jackets for a hug
      clothes smelling of weed & baccy
with recognition in a crowd
      the same orange jumper
      green striped tee
      so clothes were our bodies
with no care for glamour
      no buffing or waxing
      tom-boys no make-up
with pills in your pocket
with no money to go out
      so we stayed in
      so we stayed in

Give Me Another List

Impossible   Fascinating

Fatal   Ultimate

Cruel   Compelling

Selfish   Determined

She laid the trail of crumbs & he followed. Willingly.

    Or he laid them & she followed?

Do Not Take the Fruit of Goblin Men

Never argued with anyone like I argued with him.
Craftsman: we acted out the roles we had assigned
ourselves when I threw his stuff out of the window
or he bundled me naked into the hallway
& locked the door stoned, slender, skin
scrunched against the gloss paint door, fear of neighbours
seeing the visual proof of our ridiculousness

      & waiting in town for his gilded self
to turn up, I was still tripping from last night,
idling over a book of poems about dangerous
fruit sellers — sweet cherries!

when the dead singer
sat down at the table opposite & leant back,
read a leather-bound book of his own   I didn't speak
he smirked: it was comforting not to wait
alone & I was grateful   he was young, black
leather jacket, long hair curled on his collar
      sadness in his opacity, people walked past, I
shook with nerves in case he vanished, or if
I took my eyes away for a second he would melt
back into the ether he came from
                I desired
my boyfriend because he looked like him—
selfish, acid-introducing, arrogant, trouble-causing,
dazzling, unfaithful to me with a tiger, boyfriend:

25

another bad choice   then he got up & left,

tucking his own book into the inside

pocket of his coat: even now,

I wonder what he was reading that day.

This poem makes no sense, either use punctuation or don't use it.

Stop mixing up your ~~drugs~~ boyfriends

Describe a Picture No One Else Has Seen

It's blurred.
The colours have faded a little & there is a drawing pin
 hole in the top left. Like it was pinned to a board for the last
 twenty years. Sun sucking the intensity out of it. She's laughing,
 her eyes are crinkled in the corner. Someone just said something funny
& the photographer caught the moment she cracked up.

She's wearing a white dress with leaf patterns on it. Bangles
around her wrists, sliver, leather, friendship cotton bands, her slim
arm held up as if celebrating. Scars.

Her hair is long, straight, heavy bangs, red: the colour of a copper
plate, buried for 2000 years & then dug up from a barrow ... polished
so it burns bright. Her eyes are green. Specifically,
the colour of a piece of plucked sage.

Wait, you said her hair was the colour of burnt wood.

   Green?

The Colour of Burnt Wood

Escapism isn't really any kind of escape:
the things that haunt you follow
into the smoky corners of the club, into
bedclothes of a bed that isn't familiar.
Humans screw up, broken ones
especially; it's hard to cling to the life
buoy when the terrifying sea is choppy
& you just want to let go & drown.
It's a constant burning at the stake —
lost is a hell of a place to get back from.
When your compass is a blank disc
& you lie in a hot bath tub with a knife
on the edge & consider reasons why
you shouldn't do it, why you should stay.

Too gloomy, tell me about the prettiness again.

No. Tell me the worst thing.

The Worst Thing

The 17 year old girl sits outside the bathroom
surrounded by the perfume
of things that never get washed.
She is wearing an oversized grey jumper,
she has small hands & ankles
& her thighs are bruised.
She is reading old football mags,
junk mail & copies of the *Daily Sport*:
the girl loves to read & he has no books.
She reads the words on his posters,
the sleeves of his tape cassettes.
She reads them over again – any words will do.
He is sleeping right next door
on a mattress lay flat on the floor,
she is lonely but she dare not wake him up.
The other boys in the house tried to warn her,
they feel so sorry for her.
But hey, what can they do, they're scared of him too.
It's not a squat but it may as well be,
the landlord overlooks stuff.
Extra lads that live there & the doors smashed in.
He is four years older,
plays messed up games, soppy-tender – then he hurts.
The girl is jumped-in-deep-end romantic,
he has black curls & charisma.
She's without words.
He loves to force her, for years she said

29

he forced her. Her therapist friend said, no

he raped you & that is why you are trembling

& can't get your breath. The girl bites down

on the songbird & spits out feathers.

He's only in this poem: he doesn't deserve another

    Actually, you lied, this wasn't the worst thing

Wasted

Drinking in the park, drinking on a fake ID
Drinking cider, Thunderbirds, 20/20, Taboo
Drinking to get courage, drinking to dance
Drinking, drinking, drinking until you
Fall over & say all the wrong things
Shout, cry, get lost, kiss the wrong man
Kiss the right girl, feel nothing, drink!

Drink too much for your small frame
Drink like all the boys you hang with
Drink so much at your work drinks
You have to take some ecstasy to sober up
Drink so you have to apologise: sorry, sorry!
Drink like you are in the longhouse,
Drink because sobriety is painful, drink!

Such Lost Pretty Things

it's the young love that gilds them
burnished gold that gleams on
& on through time & songs
draws the eye of strangers
warming their hands on
that love made in long summer nights

it welded the pair to the bitter end
falling into each other
before the fame got rabid
when they were still just
a couple in love
one boy & one girl

long legged, easy grace, handsome
face — tangled, shoulder length hair
beads hanging, leather coat
the sensual mouth kissing the slender
shoulder of his little girl, her long hair
fanned on the floor as they laugh,
love making in young skins
big grins, going to make the world

explode, pleasure in everything
a smoke of weed, a swig of whiskey
drugs to make the walls kaleidoscope
more & more of this & that
& then the bigger thrill
another leap into
a deeper, darker, colder hole

& why would they jump
off a cliff like that?
what pained them is their secret to keep

Who are you talking about: tell me the real truth!

people would drift in

at different times, everyone would wait,
play pool, drink cheap beer
upstairs, at The Crown,
go & score from the bloke
who had the scar across his cheek
Tony someone? forgotten now

the Seattle singer was dead but his voice
his voice & other pine-tinged voices
played on repeat in a small town
landlocked, far from America
far from the chill Pacific North West:
this was the Shire, rolling hills
& Porcelain factory jobs

this was strange, why
we all loved punk & grunge
listening to bands in the art deco
theatre, hanging off the steps
female singer howling still
but I think
it was the dirty *drugs* honesty

The Real Truth

this phrase annoys me: what is real
what is true,
everything is filtered through bias
memories that re-arrange like landscapes

it's familiar   but something dark has grown
shading the whole left side of it all
or the unkempt, tangled bushes have been strimmed
back to grass & everything is simplified
                    she was in love
with a rock star who died, she died too

Heroin Badge

you are not supposed to boast about it
it's not cool, it's not membership
to an exclusive club

it's meeting under the arches to buy
speed & going back to the house,
wasted bodies huddled in long sleeves,
shy, wanting to keep their dignity

it's hiding it from me, it's stealing,
taking advantage of kindness
it's being drawn to guys like this
eating the blue flower
sensitive men, those with some
deep wound they were filling with dirt
it's thinking of all the ones, gone

it's recognising I was lucky no one
offered it to me, because I had pain
to blot out & I would have liked it,
it's getting out of there
it's not wearing it like a badge
to win some bizarre coolness points
it's finishing with you because you do

Smiles

Two photographs of two dead people
both beautiful, both smiling —
in black & white & some song lyrics.
It looked authentic, a snapshot of love,
but an image of fakery: unreliable narrators.
Posted online it was shared as real
& a woman in South America
had it printed onto a t-shirt; so surreal.

Did you see, the new pictures?

Such a waste, she was so young to be wasted.

So, You Got Your Rock Star Death in the End

& it wasn't glamourous or cool; no one follow/admire this.

She is as precious as a robin's egg tucked inside an old kettle.

You gave a smaller contribution than an unshed tear-drop.

How can I address this to you when you will never read it?

I thought … I thought, one day we would see each other again.

I thought, she would be able to meet you if she wanted to.

One day. Now there are no more days. I can't write this;

it was a prose poem, but it became too personal. Metaphor.

The rabbit, stripped of its fur, was a little thing with gentle

eyes & the pursuer applied the coup de grâce tenderly.

Gretel's Crumbs

          he was cool,
don't get me wrong, he was   but she was
cooler, hoarfrost in her veins perhaps, doll-like
those violet eyes & the biggest grin
she would leap in, & he would be right behind
Carey Hunter would always seek
          out the next thrill, something to wipe
away the memory of that loss   seek
& find   love street   hate street
          any club, any building, she could
score, she had a gift

I wish I could see a video of her, hear her speak.

Enough already.

(un) real woman

create a character on the role-playing game
with her name so she can kick the shit out
of the monster who got in her way
so she gets home alive
      give her music to your daughter

Mia Zapata wins

CPSIA information can be obtained
at www.ICGtesting.com
Printed in the USA
BVHW011531010222
627619BV00022B/147

9 781912 211302